HOLDING ON

Poems
for
Alex

How to measure
a season against
the calendar of
your absence?

John Berger

Cathy Sosnowsky

HOLDING ON

Poems
for
Alex

Creative Connections Publishing

National Library of Canada Cataloguing in Publication Data

Sosnowsky, Cathy, 1939-
Holding on

ISBN 1-894694-04-X

1. Grief--Poetry. I. Title.
PS8587.O84H64 2001   C811'.6 C2001-910372-7
PR9199.4.S68H64 2001

Illustrations: Alex Sosnowsky
Photographs: Sosnowsky family collection
Editing: Paul Vanderham
Cover Design: James O'Mara and Leon Phillips
Book Design: Leon Phillips
Proofreading: Bernard Shalka

First Printing: June 2001

Creative Connections Publishing
Suite 212 - 1656 Duranleau
Granville Island
Vancouver, BC • V6H 3S4
604-688-0320 • toll-free 1-877-688-0320
email: ccpublishing@axion.net
www.creativeconnectionspublishing.com

Affiliated Publishers in
Vancouver • Calgary • Milwaukee • Denver

Printed in Canada

To my son
Alexander John Sosnowsky

December 9, 1975 – December 12, 1992

Contents

Acknowledgements ix

Introduction: Grief, A Shared Journey xi

Poem for Alex's Funeral 1

River Burial 2

The Empty Room 3

The Post 4

Grief and Dreams 5

Lament 6

The First Spring 8

Hanging On 9

The Gap 10

When Bad Things Happen to Good People 11

Wait for Us 12

Alex and the Bear 13

Canned Raspberries 15

Poem for Alex's Birthday 17

Alone / Christmas Eve Afternoon / The Hotel California 18

In a Tennis Bubble 19

The Bronze Lady and the Black Balloon 20

Graduation Photos 21

Raven Talks to Woldy 22

Fall 23

Tennis, Death and Poetry   24

Beach Poem, Manzanillo   26

Sea Call   27

The Virgin of Guadalupe   28

Still Life   29

Christmas, Six Years After   30

November Poem   31

For What I Want   33

Translated from the Greek   34

Sometimes   35

A Love Story   36

Thoughts at the Mountain   37

A Man's Grief   38

Osprey   40

Beach Havens   42

Notes   44

Acknowledgements

I would like to thank the many friends who loved Alex and me enough to read these poems in their earliest, most painful forms: Brian, Carol, Margie, Ruth, Elizabeth, Sharon, James, Kate, Helen . . . .

I am also grateful to the many encouraging poet-mentors I have been privileged to work with: Roger Semmens, Paula Meehan, Olga Broumas, and, through the *Capilano Review*'s Writing Practices Program, bill bissett, Sharon Thesen, and Don McKay. I'm particularly grateful to Don for releasing me from my obsession with rewriting. "Don't worry if every one of these poems is not perfect," he said. "In some cases, life takes precedence over art." He advised me to leave my early, blunt poems as they were—unadulterated expressions of feeling.

Special thanks to my fellow members of the Poets Anonymous Collective, Jennifer Scott and Carol Ogden. Their supportive critical comments helped shape many of the later poems included in this volume. More importantly, looking forward to workshopping with them kept me writing.

Alex, too, has contributed to this collection, not only by inspiring the poems, but also by supplying the artwork. All drawings are from Alex's sketchbooks or journals.

And Woldy, thank you for holding me.

The working title of this collection of poems was *Hanging On*, a phrase that captured, I thought, my desperation as a grieving mother. But when my friend James O'Mara was experimenting with the cover design, he unconsciously retitled the work *Holding On*. As I was looking over his proposed layouts, it took me a while to notice his mistake. When I did, and mentioned it to him, James apologized for his oversight, but added that he thought the tenderness implied in "holding" suited the cover image of mother and child better than my original word choice.

If this collection contained only poems from my first two years of grief, "hanging on" would, in fact, be the appropriate title. Like many parents whose child predeceases them, I wanted to die myself when we lost our son. In those first years of grief I was barely hanging on to life, and struggling to hang on to my sanity. I desperately wanted to hang on to Alex too; I couldn't believe that my golden child was dead. I read self-help books about grieving, and dutifully wrote the recommended good-bye letters in an attempt to "let go."

But I couldn't let go. Alex kept reappearing—in dreams, in the stories of his friends, and in various forms of birds. Alex was always a bird lover, and as a little boy told people he wanted to be "an ornithologist" when he grew up. ("A what?" they'd say.)

Even more so, Alex remained with me as my poetic muse. The second morning after his death I woke from a half-sleep with two lines of poetry echoing in my head: "He came to us in the dead of winter,/ Lighting the darkness with his smile." I had to get up, get to my desk, and write them down. Other lines followed almost automatically, and together they became "Poem for Alex's Funeral," the first poem in this collection.

During my first year of grieving I wrote over 140 poems. Every blossom, every falling leaf was imbued with meaning, and I had to write it down—however unclear that "meaning" was. Writing poetry was a form of therapy, and continued to be a way of expressing my depression, my confusion, and my surprising moments of joy in the years that followed. The poems selected here were written over an eight-year period. I am now aware that their style changed as I became more conscious of poetry as form, and their content lightened as I reconnected with the larger world around me. Putting this collection together, in fact, has been another significant step on my journey, another source of joy. Like T.S. Eliot I have rejoiced, "having to construct something upon which to rejoice."

One of the reasons I decided to publish these poems is that I remember how the reading of the grief journeys of others helped me through my early pain. I could read about nothing else, and was grateful that others had recorded, and were willing to share, their grief stories: C. S. Lewis, Rainer Maria Rilke, Dietrich Bonhoeffer, Nicholas Wolterstorff, Kuki Gellman . . . . It was a comfort to learn that wiser minds than my own had gone through the same questioning, the same insanity, the same self-pity, and the same longing.

I found another means of sharing my grief burden when I stumbled into my first meeting of The Compassionate Friends. My involvement with our local chapter of this international self-help organization of bereaved parents proved to be a saving grace. At TCF meetings, once a month, I still sit with others who have lost their children, sharing memories, pain and anger, crying and even laughing together. In my first year, I sobbed through every meeting. Now, eight years into my journey, I act as a facilitator and greeter at meetings, and edit our chapter's newsletter. At The Compassionate Friends retreats I have given workshops on "writing your way through grief." By helping others I have experienced healing myself.

Healing has also taken place through the great forces of nature and myth. The sea, in particular, has sustained me, even though, during my suicide period, it was my choice as a means of death. As Freud and Jung assure us, the sea is a universal symbol of the subconscious, and a journey to sea often has archetypal implications. Because we spent every summer on our sailboat with Alex from the time he was seven months old, the sea for me is also the setting for particularly cherished memories. My husband and I believe Alex became the daring white water kayaker he was at sixteen because of his early love of stormy waters. His ashes, released in his favorite river, the Mamquam, are now travelling the world's ocean currents.

Although a native shaman presided over the releasing of Alex's ashes, I had been attending a Christian church before Alex died, and have continued to do so after his death. Our Presbyterian minister, Ian Victor, knew and loved the boy whose funeral he conducted. Ian said exactly the right thing when he came to our home at one a.m., an hour after the young police officer had delivered the bludgeoning news. Ian held my husband's and my hand— Woldy, Ian, and I sitting side by side on Alex's empty bed. I am thankful that Ian did not say, "You'll have to accept this. It's God's will," but rather kept repeating, "I can't believe it. I can't believe it." He said what we felt in this first sharing of our pain.

What I also couldn't believe—besides the fact that Alex was dead—was that I'd ever see my son again. Ian had to assure me, that night and for months and years after, that *he believed* I would. I found comfort in the strength of his faith. The question of life after death is one I repeatedly struggled with in my earlier poems. It was not until seven years after Alex died, after I was no longer struggling, that I was gifted with the peaceful vision of transcendence described in the poem "Thoughts at the Mountain."

Another significant source of healing for me was my identification with the Virgin Mary, in particular, the dark Madonnas of the world. Mary, too, lost her only begotten son, and at times I seemed to confuse Alex with Christ. On one of our many attempted "geographical cures" after Alex's death, a summer trip to Europe, I lit candles before images of the Virgin in churches throughout England, France, Belgium, Switzerland and Italy. Each of the effigies of Mary had its own personality, yet each represented the grieving mother. These homages provided me with a symbolic lesson on the universality of suffering.

In reducing an eight-year grief journey to a selection of thirty-five poems, I have necessarily omitted some aspects of my life during that time: my relationship with my husband, my relationship to my remaining children, and my relationship to my work. The different ways in which men and women express their grief and the alienating effect of child loss on a marriage are topics that often come up at TCF meetings. Each parent has had a special relationship with the child who died, and, in a way, has suffered a different loss. Although my husband Woldy and

I have stayed together, and mourned together, we have also felt our aloneness. "A Love Story" and "A Man's Grief," both recent poems, indicate for me an emergence from the self-absorption of my grief into a stronger appreciation of married love.

A question often asked of bereaved parents is "Do you have other children?" Yes, we have Tanya and Michael whom we adopted, at the ages of four and six, when Alex was eight. Both were profoundly grieved by their brother's death. I have written poems to them and about them, but those belong in another volume.

When I returned to college teaching a few weeks after Alex's death, I made no attempt to hide my loss from students and colleagues. Fortunately, my work, the teaching of literature and writing, invited the sharing of feelings. Colleagues were quite accepting when I cried in the halls in response to their "How are you doing?" They lent me their shoulders, and I was able to carry on. Students came to my office to talk to me about their own losses. One of them told me this Zen story about grief: A mother who had lost her only child to death went to see the Buddha. "Oh, Buddha, you can do anything," she said. "Please restore my son to me." The Buddha set her a quest: "Go to the neighbouring village. Knock on every door. If you can find one home that has not experienced grief, come and tell me of it. Then I will restore your son to life." The woman knocked and knocked. She found no family that had not experienced loss. Instead, she heard many sorrow-filled stories. She returned to the Buddha to thank him for his help. She did not regain her son, but instead was granted enlightenment.

Although these poems for Alex represent a particular loss and retell a personal journey, none of us is immune to grief.

He came to us in the dead of winter,
Lighting the darkness with his smile.
He strode through our world,
Giant feet carrying grace.
Roaring down rivers, climbing cliffs,
Drawing, dreaming, kissing, laughing,
His best belovéd: a small green bird.

He left us in the dead of winter,
Broken ribbed—he really couldn't fly.
We mourn him, broken too.

We needed an Indian
to scatter the ashes.
Our own black-robed priest,
the church and the coffin
oppressed his light spirit.

We needed the river,
the clean cedar branches,
a drum with a heartbeat,
ochre paint for the eye
on the Never-Sink kayak

overturned now and pierced
(an eye for the fish
keeps them safe from the dead).

To the sounds of the drum
and the screeching of eagles,
we let our son go,
gave him back to the river
whose constant commotion

had quickened his soul.
We needed the Shaman
slow moving   deep seeing
to transform the ashes:

boy into man, man into river.
Now his ashes are flowing
through all of our world.

suspended

the broad-winged bird does not stir

above the breathless bed

black baseball mit   red haki-sac

lie limp upon the desk

boxes of colored boxes: mad turtles

fighting rabbits   tough milkmen

closed shut from laughter

chewed pencils   broken sticks of charcoal

image-spent in the brown desk drawer

Led Zeppelin   Dire Straits   Paul Simon

trapped   in soundless plastic

a poster crackles

dangles from the wall

Mommy wonders   should she fix it?

a stone's throw from the slow
      grey river
half-hidden
      by poplar and fern
a silver post stands
by a pond
where salmon spawn

gravel trucks rattle by
    unaware
      of the sleeping youth
    unaware
      of the Mother's Day
      forget-me-nots
making new roots
    in this old soil

let me tell you about grief:

a bathtub full of stinging nettle
a deep dark hole
a chasm

your body: aching   bruised   heavy
wants to lie down
fall down

but the hole is full of rats
no sweet oblivion

only regret   rage
self-pity

oh let us bathe in stinging nettle!
the pain will be distracting

those surface itches
better than the hole

where despair waits
a ravenous rat

to feed upon
our sweetest dreams

One dark night in December,
death and poetry
entered our house,
shaping my lips forever
in a song of lament.

I could not cry alone,
had to shout my sorrow,
hear it ring among the aisles
of canned tomatoes, boxes of rice
frozen burritos—Alex's favorite.

Rilke cried with me.
His voice reaching the angels'
hierarchies. Sure, even if
one of them pressed him
to his heart, he would be consumed.

Beauty, he said, *is the beginning
of terror.*   Trees turn to flame,
birds to wingéd gods,
each crying my son's name:
Alex!   Alex!   Alex!

my long awaited, only begotten
one. Part boy,   part man,
lean, sunbrown, loping walk
teasing grin,   a trickster,
his means of death a joke

almost: he fell through a seam
of a bubble (step on a crack, break
your mother's back) landed on his head,
staining the tennis court's floor
deep vermilion.

He let out a comic book scream,
his friend said, falling easily
after him,   the bubble collapsing
slowly on the pair
Jon frantically

pumping air into Alex's bleeding
mouth,   punching the policeman
who said his friend was dead,
his youth bruised by one night's
folly, the whining dog now quiet.

Oh God, what do I do
with my unfinished love?
Ann Weems cries.
We form a chorus, women in black,
calling for our disappeared.

Some scratch their pain on paper,
Kuki Gellman, dreaming of Africa,
myself, compelled: each falling
leaf, an Icarus,
each blossom, a cut off dream.

I would like to fling my voice out like a cloth
over the fragments of your death, and keep
pulling at it until it is torn to pieces,
and all my words would have to walk around
shivering, in the tatters of that voice,

if lament were enough.

who ever thought blossoms
could hurt?

We're trying to hang on
to this elusive child,

cementing a bronze plaque
to a giant grey rock
(the river rushing below it),

enlarging an earlier image,
framing it in silver:
a five-year-old, running, laughing,
his flying feet splashing drops of sun
light across a pool-drenched beach,

naming a star in the heavens:
Alex Sosnowsky, number 21729
(forgetting that the steadfastness
is only an illusion),

printing words on paper
seeing if black and white
can still, distill,   his spirit.

But Alex keeps running,
keeps flowing,
keeps laughing.

It may be,
we might have to,
let him go.

Nothing can fill the gap,
said Bonhoeffer, in prison,
shut off from those he loved,
but not from God.

Although the gap may fill,
said Freud, *it nevertheless
remains something else.*

Both agree, the gap is good.

My gap aches, yawns open, hollow,
black.   Four months of tears
have not begun to fill it.

I need Donne's oceans.
I need God's grace.

The title of a book,
written by a rabbi.
His two-year-old son
was destined to be old,
fast,
much too fast.
Progeria, it's called.
He died an old man,
aged fourteen.

Kushner also writes of the Holocaust:
God, he says, was on the side
of the sufferers, but dare not
intervene, else they wouldn't
be free.

We're all free,
free to fall,
as Milton's God puts it.
Free to suffer.

Our son fell freely.
We could not stop him.
God could not stop him.

Now we are left
to free ourselves,
to free ourselves
from Alex's fall.

wait for us, Alex
    but where?
in the river's rushing water?
in the star-sprinkled sky?
in the bosom of Abraham?

or, if you remain only
in those you left behind
you'll soon be off:
    mountain climbing with Kelsey
    cycling Australia with Jon
    horseback riding with Tanya
you might even walk
around the world with Courtney

you'll be making funny faces
in Emily's and Amy's art
playing tennis with Cole and me

and when we're gone?

will Emily's children tell
how their mother came to have
your great-grandmother's
gold-frosted tea cup?

teacups break, Alex!
    rivers are safer
    skies are vaster
    Abraham's bosom more ample

wait for us there, Alex

Six months after my son's death,
I found his diary:
"Look out! There's a mountain!"
he yelled to the three pilots
on his cockpit ride to Mazatlan.

In Alex's journal, too, were dreams of rescue—
he and Jon rescuing friends by hang-glider,
his dad saving him twice,
once from a shark, once from a bear.

That night I fell asleep smiling.

Then Alex appeared in my dream,
eating bread and honey
on a mountain, with his dad.

"Look out for bears!" I shouted,
and one appeared.

"Give it your honey Alex!"
but the bear's paws had already
encircled the startled boy
ready to claw his soft young face.

The rescuer dad sat paralyzed,
my calls for help could not be heard
by Alex's friends across the valley,
the warden with the gun—too far away!

I turned back to face the torn image,
but saw, instead, a gentle bear
meander down the mountain.

So much like the dream I had 26 years ago—
my dying dad helpless
on my bedroom floor,
a cougar attacking the house,
myself flying from door to door
frantically locking,

only to find, on return to my room,
a giant golden cat
asleep beside my dad.

last night I ate
        the raspberries
I canned for Alex

a few months ago
        just to see them
    made me cry

sweet and bright
        soft and pitty
  these basement berries
keepers of lost sunshine
taste just like the berries
my mother used to can
        for me

They called him Aleroo,
Oh, he wore a giant shoe!
He could kayak over falls
And dance all night at balls.
When his laughter filled the room,
The girls would fairly swoon,
But his greatest love of all
Was a parrot who would call
"Kuwack! Kuwack! He's home!"
And then his mouth would foam
Till he filled it with burritos,
Then he'd say, "Oh that was neato!
Let's watch cartoons on TV
Homework can wait for me.
Once I have won my fame,
No one will ever blame
You, Mom, for having spoilt me,
They'll write me in their poetry!"

Paul Simon's soft voice rings caressive:
hearts and bones, hearts and bones

a bright-breasted bird   alight
lights outside my broad-leafed window
cocks his head
         bobs it   in tune

is it you, Alex?
come for Christmas, did you?

"Hola,   my baby Jesús."

Costa Rica
December 24, 1993

she tries to hit the ball within the lines
it used to be easy
now   the yellow ball
flies too high   too far
no longer obedient
to the player's will
the player's skill
she paces   volleys   serves
panting in plastic air
all sounds are blurred
she dare not pause
dare not look up
confront the false grey sky
if she does
she too will fall
like her son
imprinted
on the cold green floor

A bronze lady sits on a park bench,
waiting for a bus that never comes.

Her name is "Search." She's looking
for her glasses, holding the empty case
suspended over her gaping bag.

No one tells her they're on her head,
instead, they give her flowers, take
her photo with their friends,
to send to Tokyo.

I worry about her as I pass,
going in the opposite direction
on my way to work.

Today someone gave her
a black balloon.

In silver frames, Emily and Jon,
black garbed, well combed and
serious, are cheered on by a tow-headed
rascal in overalls.

He's not mean spirited,
doesn't begrudge them graduating
without him. He's graduated
already. Flown upwards

to test our higher wisdom,
and now he laughs and watches
our pompous ceremonies, his mother,
a guest on stage, endlessly crying.

"Cheer up!" says Alex. "You, too,
will reach the higher plane,
and then we all can celebrate,
together."

Smelling of musk oil and sweat,
he swings the pick into the rockbound
earth. Alone. The forest echoes.

But wait. . . there's someone talking,
someone squawking:
   right on Dad!
     squawk   squawk
   keep swinging Dad!
     squawk   squawk
   I'm watching Dad
     squawk   squawk
   black wings shining Dad
     squawk   squawk

   watch me flying Dad.

Hemming Bay
August, 1994

now the shadows that follow us
are crisper   more defined   longer
        hard to ignore

on the tennis court   another player
mimics my movements
south of the net   my darker self
reaches the ball before me

the ball too is newly defined
vibrant yellow against the deeper blue
it hangs suspended in mid throw
        I hesitate to swing

outside the white lines
in the shade of late summer trees
the dew never melts
the court's red borders
turn a slimish green

when the ball strays
you must walk carefully
you must slow down

    winter's coming

        don't fall

she keeps writing poems about tennis
no one in her poetry class plays tennis
they think the yellow ball is the sun
her poetry teacher thought
"sun" was a pun on "son"
(she hadn't used the word "sun")

some of these non-playing poets
haven't seen a tennis bubble
anyway, who would believe
a boy could die that way
falling through a tear in a bubble?

and who could understand
the pain of a mother
who can't play tennis
without seeing her son's dead body
lying on the cold green court

"maybe you should fictionalize
his means of death"
her poetry teacher suggested

yes: he died trying to fly
he died racing raging rapids
he died rescuing a kitten
drowning in a lake
he died climbing a mountain
—had almost reached the top
he died smothered in my arms
as I tried to save him
from an incurable illness
Oh Alex, did you have to climb a bubble?
wouldn't this earth's solid ground
do, for you?

you always wanted to be an eagle
your art teacher said you were reaching
for the stars

Moonlit on the balcony,
she listens to the waves,
hearing echoes of Arnold—
his *eternal note of sadness.*

Her world too has lost its measure,
her son's ashes now—perhaps—
part of this booming sea,
his child's voice barely heard

above its roar. "Help push nuclear
weapons out of this world!" the
golden-haired six-year-old chants,
sending beached bombs to drift

—harmless—back to sea.
She hears his first sentence echo
across a quiet bay in Desolation
Sound: "Mommy, go BOOM!"

Sees herself cannonballing overboard,
her laughter erupting in a watery volcano.

Now, beside this warmer ocean, wishing
again to drown her deathless sorrow,
she wonders, "What does it take,
to go boom?"

she has been drawn by the sea to suicide
its soothing salt   eternal motion
flashes of silver
     punctuating darkness
single-minded amoeba
     never needing direction

full fathoms five!
where lost souls ring
and coral gardens bloom all year

beneath the waves and changing light
  lie darkness   depth
       in sight
       insight

We climbed the sundried pyramids,
admired the stone Chac-Mool
(lying back, smiling,
 his tummy a resting place
 for torn-out hearts).

Now it was the Virgin's turn.
We'd pay a visit,
see what the conquerors
(those steel-clad men)
had to offer.

To replace the burning sacrifices
(to replace them with their own).

They'd built a church around her
(little lady dressed in blue).

Millions crawled to see her,
crawled on bleeding knees
(little lady dressed in blue).

Don't be afraid she'd told the farmer.
Look, I'm dark like you.
See, I too have suffered
(little lady dressed in blue).

The soldiers killed my baby,
nailed him up for all to see.

No more need of bloody offerings,
no more need of shiny swords.
Come, let us cry together—
my cloak will keep you warm.

Still Life

pink tulips stretch
plastic Mary prays
white candle waves
and Alex smiles
in blue

I don't remember the first Christmas.
Thirteen days without my son
—who was counting?
I was numb.

The second Christmas we ran away
to beaches fringed with jungles
(the monkeys were distracting).
Midnight mass in Spanish:
"un hombre único"
Christ or Alex?
Only begotten son.

The sixth season without him,
friends are pleased to hear me laugh.
They don't mention his name,
afraid, this late, to see my pain.
Even I hesitate to say it:
Alex   Alex   Alex . . .
sounding more and more like an echo

Now my fear is that he'll fade,
my own laughter, drowning his.

In the dark days of November,
my thoughts turn towards my dead:
father, mother, uncle, cousin,
our long-limbed son, our Alex,
who never had a chance
to become a man.

Ghosts of unknown soldiers
come marching by:
Sassoon, Owen, Graves,
who wrote their pain in mud
and turned a young girl's heart
forever towards poetry.

At night November storms
shake our thin-paned shelter
and raging trees cry out
like Lear—a king's despair—
his riches turned to rags.

I think about the eagle's nest,
a thatchwork of broken twigs
fifty feet high and six feet wide
and wonder,   will it hold?

For distraction, I pick up a play.
Characters worry about the millennium.
One recalls flagellants of the last one
beating themselves raw—imitating Christ.

"Why couldn't they imitate Jesus
when he was happy?"
the young brassy Island Girl proposes.
"Why didn't they go lie in a manger
and say, 'Look, I'm Jesus'–
at least they'd have been comfortable."

Right on Janine!   A December poem:
why don't we each curl up in a bed of straw
and listen to the animals,
happy in their fur coats,
purring and barking their way
to Heaven.

I'd give you my Italian roast coffee
from the shop on Second Avenue
I'd give you my eagle earrings
from Umista Gallery in Alert Bay
I'd give you the 140 poems
I wrote in my first year of grief
I'd give you Missy's luminous green feathers
blue at their tips
I'd give you my cracked Mennonite desk
its red surface fading
I'd give you my black puppy
with worried brown eyebrows
I'd give you our tugboat
its bright plastic dishes
Scrabble by candles
a rocking pillow for bed
if I could, I would give you
my love for the dead

I miss you
return to me again
in dreams
whisper soft and low
where you've been   what you did
stay longer
give me a kiss
I'll find your yellow tugboat
you can take it with you
all your dreams upon it
we'll sail away
others will miss us
family   friends   cat   dog
we'll be happy alone together
watch the others far away
"Good luck!"   we'll call out
"Love each other well
—don't forget!"

sometimes I go deep into the forest
looking for light
finding none, I panic
want to turn back
but I've already lost my way
I look for animal tracks
to lead me
to a cave for shelter
or perhaps towards still water
fresh, clear and deep
reflecting there
a lone star's light

A Love Story

love was a song about a jet plane
love was a liver sausage sandwich
love rode a bus to Marrakech
singing every song it ever knew
love bore a dead baby in a London hospital
wore an Afghanistan wedding dress
with a crown of daisies
sailed a small boat
a salmon stealing its first fishing rod
while we read the instructions
love became a pretty baby
jolly jumping from the boom
running races in the school yard
delivering papers with his parrot
making cartoon movies of singing crows
climbing sea cliffs to jump
rainbowlike, at noon
climbing, once, too high
falling far too soon
and falling again
and again
and again

love carries on
bearing our dead son within and between us
listening for his song
seeing the chip in his front tooth
scar over his right eye
callous on thumb

love doesn't let go

wind lifts powdery snow skyward
like angel wings

hidden still, the rising sun
haloes the peak

piercing white against blue

one black midnight
at the base of this mountain
while I slept

my son fell

his spirit left his body
here
here, at this mountain

did it rise like the snow
barely visible in darkness?

or did it wait for morning light
to leap upwards?

Whistler
December, 1999

It was almost Christmas
when our son died.
My husband's sobs
shook the funeral chapel.
It hurt, he said.

He took refuge in rocks.
Rolled them into the church
to rest the kayak on,
an unclaimed gift beneath
the tinselled tree.

Later at the river
he put rocks inside the boat.
The boy, no longer coffined,
no longer flesh,
would not need craft or paddle
to navigate one last time
his favorite rapids.

The fish would wonder
at this painted diamond,
weighted down
in their spawning channel,
unmoved
even in winter floods.

The gulls screeched
as it sank
in a whirling cloud
of flowers and ash.

In the spring he trekked upriver,
drill, ladder, cement in hand,
to find the largest rock
beneath the falls
for his son's plaque.

A gravestone, a grassy plot,
too tame
to hold his grief,

the river itself
not strong enough
to cry his tears.

I

A broad-winged bird, cardboard
feathered, each one meticulously
etched, cut out and glued,

hangs still, suspended
over the empty bed,
its patchwork quilt, neatly

tucked for months now,
its only occupant a Santa-
capped Sylvester, plushly

grinning in black and white,
as if he'd swallowed
the osprey's trout.

II

Alex's first kayak, handmade
too, was named "Never Sink"
by him, after the

Little Captain's ship in
Little Captain and Marinka
(who made great pancakes);

bought it himself with paper-
route money he collected,
green parrot on his shoulder,

but the maker, Walter,
said the model's trade
name was really *Osprey*.

III
In Alex's summer journal,
written three years before
he died, he drew two baby

ospreys peeking from
their spiky nest, sixty feet
above the lake—*They*

were the best part!
he wrote.

IV
Suk 'yu was the name
of the shaman who blessed
Alex's ashes as we fed

them to his favorite river
just before we let the gashed
kayak go—Suk 'yu, cleansing

our home with cedar branches,
paused beside the bed,
studying the bird. *My*
name, he said, *means osprey.*

As the tide of grief goes down,
new beaches are revealed.

Their sand, it's true,
is wet,
and barnacles protrude.

But wear your rubber shoes
(hot pink would be preferred).
Step dainty on the shore:

a storm-thrown log
will give you rest.

Now sit and sun yourself,
and dream of those you love.

Notes

Poem for Alex's Funeral: As mentioned in the introduction, this poem was composed almost automatically. It was only recently that another poet pointed out to me that my first line echoes the first line of W. H. Auden's "In Memory of W. B. Yeats." The automatic writing, then, came from a good source.

The Post: My brother-in-law, Vic Sosnowsky, hewed a simple post to mark the place on the river where we held the ashes ceremony. On the post Vic carved symbols to represent the things Alex loved: a kayak, an eagle, a musical note, a paint brush, a pen, a wave, a sunset. It's a totem pole, of sorts.

Lament: "Beauty is the beginning of terror" is from Rainer Maria Rilke's *The Duino Elegies*. "Oh God, what do I do with my unfinished love?" is from Ann Weems' *Psalms of Lament*, written after the death of her twenty-one-year-old son. Kuki Gellman's fourteen-year-old son died in Africa, poisoned by a bite from his pet snake. His death and her mourning are described in her book *I Dreamed of Africa*. "Women in black" alludes to the women in Latin America who gather in public squares to hold protest vigils for their "disappeared" children and spouses. "I would like to fling my voice . . . if lament were enough" is from Rilke's *Requiem*.

The Gap: Dietrich Bonhoeffer, a Lutheran minister, was imprisoned for taking part in a plot against Hitler, and hung two days before Liberation. I was introduced to his words just one week after Alex's death, at the funeral of Jon Furberg, a poet and colleague who later appeared to me in a dream to tell me that he and Alex were reading poetry together. "Donne's oceans" refers to John Donne's Holy Sonnet #5 in which he asks God to save him from his own despair and disbelief by pouring "new seas" in his eyes.

When Bad Things Happen to Good People: Rabbi Harold Kushner's book addresses the anger felt by many newly bereaved, and explores the theological questions raised by brutal and meaningless deaths. John Milton's *Paradise Lost* tackles the same question of the meaning of suffering.

Poem for Alex's Birthday: At the suggestion of one of Alex's friends, we decided to hold a party for Alex on the first birthday after his death. I wrote this poem, celebrating his life, and printed it on the back of a collage of photos to give to his friends. The playfulness of this piece still astounds me. I sense that Alex wrote the poem, not me.

The Bronze Lady and the Black Balloon: Vancouver readers should recognize this lady, a life-size and life-like statue sitting on the north side of Georgia Street just before the entrance to Stanley Park. When I first saw her, I had not yet visited the famous black Madonna of Einseideln (Switzerland) or the dark Virgin of Guadalupe (Mexico), but like them she seemed to embody my pain.

Raven Talks to Woldy: The setting here is the wilderness cooperative on East Thurlow Island (just north of Campbell River) that we bought into when Alex was only two. Woldy and his brother Vic (also a shareholder) have been working on our cabin there since Alex died. Several of Alex's friends have spent some summer weeks helping—acting as substitute sons. But Woldy feels Alex's presence there most when he is alone. The cover photo, incidently, was taken at Hemming Lake on East Thurlow Island.

Beach Poem, Manzanillo: In Matthew Arnold's poem "Dover Beach," the speaker, depressed by the loss of religious faith, hears the eternal note of sadness in the sound of the sea. "Help push nuclear weapons out of this world" is a slogan six-year-old Alex picked up on one of the many "Walks for Peace" that I took him on.

November Poem: The play referred to is *2000*, by Joan MacLeod. Joan, now a well-known Canadian playwright, was once my student at Langara College.